SAMMY

SAMMY
The Classroom Guinea Pig

ALIX BERENZY

McGraw Hill SRA

Columbus, OH

To all my guinea pigs, then and now

Special thanks to the children and staff
of the McGlynn Learning Center

Reprinted by arrangement with Henry Holt and Company, LLC

Copyright © 2005 by Alix Berenzy

Library of Congress Cataloging-in-Publication Data
Berenzy, Alix.
Sammy the classroom guinea pig / Alix Berenzy.—1st ed.
p.   cm.
Summary: Ms. B and her students try to understand what is bothering Sammy, the classroom guinea pig.
[1. Guinea pigs—Fiction.   2. Schools—Fiction.] 1. Title
PZ7.B4485Sam 2005   [E]—dc22   2004010136
Designed by Patrick Collins

The artist used pastel and colored pencil to create the illustrations for this book.

SRAonline.com

Printed in Mexico.

Send all inquiries to this address:
SRA/McGraw-Hill
4400 Easton Commons
Columbus, OH 43219

ISBN: 978-0-07-610895-4
MHID: 0-07-610895-3

2 3 4 5 6 7 8 9 RRM 13 12 11 10 09 08

Sammy had his own little house. Inside was a soft blue sock. He liked to take naps on it. The sock had a hole in it, but Sammy didn't mind.

The house had two doors—one to run in and one to run out. Sometimes he ran in the "out" door and out the "in" door. Sometimes he slept on the roof.

Sammy felt safe knowing he had a place to hide.

Sammy had a big cage to scamper about in. His food bowl was always filled with fresh guinea pig pellets. He had hay to chew on, water to drink, and a round block of salt to lick.

Sammy liked his home.

Sammy couldn't read a clock, but he always knew when Ms. B, the teacher, would arrive.

Every morning she brought him a treat, but today she was late.

"WHEEP!" Sammy squeaked in greeting when she finally appeared in the doorway.

"Yes, yes. I hear you, Sammy," said Ms. B. She was thinking of all the things she had to do. She hurriedly offered him a piece of carrot.

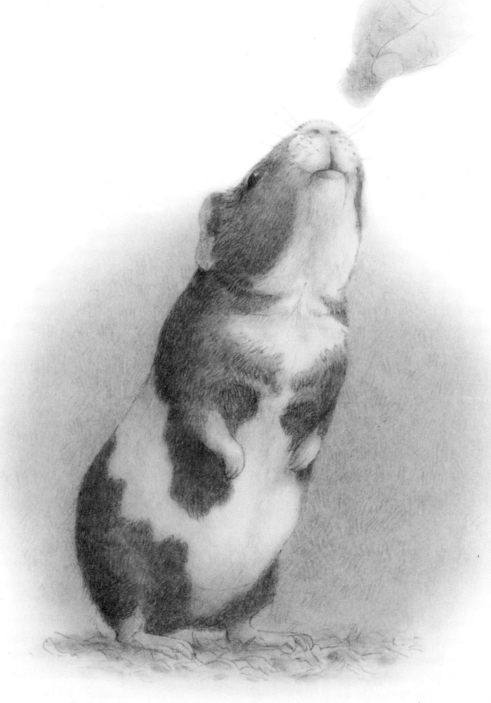

Sammy stood up on his hind legs—a difficult
trick for a guinea pig—to take the carrot.

Guinea pigs have individual tastes. Sammy liked many kinds of fruits and vegetables. Ms. B's class had learned that Sammy's favorite treat of all was cantaloupe rind.

Like most guinea pigs, he loved freshly cut grass.
In warm weather the children would bring him a
great bunch—sometimes with dandelions. They
were careful, though, not to bring him grass from the
roadside (where it could be polluted by cars or other
animals) or from a lawn treated with chemicals.

Sammy heard the voices of the children in the hall. They burst into the classroom, all talking loudly.

"Wheep! Wheep!" cried Sammy happily, adding to the din.

"Everybody settle down!" cried Ms. B.

Soon all the students were sitting in their seats
and watching Ms. B write on the blackboard.
Sammy watched too.

But as the lesson began, Sammy felt something
bothering him.

It bothered him more and more.

And more.

At last he could contain it no longer.

"WHEEEP!" he shrieked at the top of his lungs.

He sprang onto the roof of his house.

"WHEEEP! WHEEEP!" he cried again.

He leaped off and began to run, kicking wood shavings everywhere.

Ms. B stopped writing on the blackboard.

"For heaven's sakes!" she exclaimed. "What's the matter, Sammy?"

"WHEEEP! WHEEEP!" he squealed, speeding in circles around the cage.

Another burst of shavings fell to the floor. All the children turned around in their seats.

"What's the *matter*, Sammy?" they cried.

Ms. B and her students gathered around the cage. Sammy stopped scurrying and let the teacher pick him up. She lifted him with two hands, careful to support his heavy hindquarters.

Sammy found himself nose to nose with the teacher.

"What *is* the matter?" she demanded.

"WHEEEP!" Sammy shrieked.

Everyone loved Sammy and was worried.

"Is he sick?" asked Robbie.

"When guinea pigs don't feel well, they usually sit quietly with their fur puffed up," Ms. B explained. "His appetite is good. There's no wetness around his eyes or nose, which would also tell us if he were sick. He looks fine to me," she said, mystified.

"Is he afraid of something?" asked Eric.

"If Sammy were frightened, his instincts would tell him to run into his house and be very quiet. So I don't think he's afraid," the teacher reasoned. "I've taught you to talk softly and be gentle when you play with him. That way he won't be afraid of us. He will think of us as his friends."

"Maybe something is hurting him, Ms. B!" said Lisa, worried.

"Well, let's take a look," responded the teacher.

Sammy felt himself being lowered onto a table. Ms. B lifted up each of his little ears and looked into them. He felt her fingers parting his fur to reveal his skin.

He wished she would scratch him under the chin instead—he liked that.

"Do you see any red marks or bald spots?" she asked the class. "That would tell us if Sammy had a skin problem. Now *that* could make him upset."

But Sammy's skin looked perfectly healthy.

"Because we keep his cage nice and clean, it's unlikely he would have that problem. I can't imagine why he was screaming so," the teacher confessed.

Sammy decided he didn't like them looking through his fur anymore. He began to make unhappy noises—small irritated squeals and squeaks.

"Will he bite?" asked Tynisha, nervously.

"Most guinea pigs don't bite," replied Ms. B. "They bite only if they are very frightened."

She let Sammy go, and he immediately stopped
complaining. He began to waddle along the tabletop,
sniffing the surface.

"*Whutt! Whutt-whutt-whutt-whutt-whutt!*" Sammy
chuckled as he went.

"That's his exploring sound," said Ms. B. Sammy
was enjoying himself. He liked to explore new things.

Sammy made his way to Maria and touched
her nose with his.

"That's how guinea pigs recognize and greet
each other," explained Ms. B.

"*DOOT! Dutt-dutt-DEET-doot!*" Sammy
burbled in soft musical tones.

"That means he's happy," she said.

Sammy was glad when Maria picked him up and cuddled him. Her sweater was soft and warm.

"Ms. B, I think I know what's wrong with Sammy," Maria said.

"I think it's because today is Monday."

"*What?!*" everyone exclaimed.

"Sammy was alone all weekend," Maria explained. "I think he's glad to see us. He wants our attention. That's all."

Ms. B studied the little guinea pig.

"Sammy!" she said sternly. "Is this true? Is *that* what's the matter?"

Maria set Sammy down on the table, and everyone gathered closer. Sammy felt someone scratch his chin. He scrunched up his nose in pleasure.

"Doot! Deet! Dutt!" he chuckled happily.
All his friends were back!

Facts About
Guinea Pigs

+ Guinea pigs have a "language" of at least eleven different sounds.

+ Their cry of "Wheep!" is used almost exclusively to communicate with humans.

+ Guinea pigs are highly social animals; in the wild they live in close-knit "clans."

+ A guinea pig living alone will form a close bond with its owners. (If a guinea pig is left alone much of the time, it should be given a companion pig.)

+ All guinea pigs have individual personalities. The more attention and stimulation a guinea pig receives, the more its unique personality will blossom.